LOVE
FLOWS

Grow
In
Love

LOVE
FLOWS

"Love Never Fails"

LOVE IS
BLIND

LOVE ME
AS I LOVE
YOU!
MIRIAM

PRESENT
MIRIAM TEXIDOR

Dance With Me
MiriamTexidor

I ♥ Life
MIRIAM TEXIDOR

Miriam Texidor

BLOOM

PLANT FLOWERS OF HOPE

MIRIAM

MIRIAM

TRUST THE
YOURSELF

MIRIAM

Coloring takes us away from the stress of life and gives us such a calming relaxing feeling. "It helps us get into our happy place."
Each page is hand drawn and signed by the artist and then uploaded to create the coloring book. Since, it's been designed, and hand drawn by the artist, once its colored it can be displayed as an art piece.

.

Produced and designed by Artist Miriam Texidor
Deltona, Florida 32738
Email: miriamtexidor@gmail.com
Find me @ www.facebook.com/justcolormyworld
www.justcolormyworld.com